DATE DUE

When, Jen?

by Marie Powell

illustrated by Amy Cartwright

amicus
readers

1

amicus readers

Say Hello to Amicus Readers.

You'll find our helpful dog, Amicus, chasing a ball—to let you know the reading level of a book.

1

Learn to Read

Frequent repetition, high frequency words, and close photo-text matches introduce familiar topics and provide ample support for brand new readers.

2

Read Independently

Some repetition is mixed with varied sentence structures and a select amount of new vocabulary words are introduced with text and photo support.

3

Read to Know More

Interesting facts and engaging art and photos give fluent readers fun books both for reading practice and to learn about new topics.

Amicus Readers are published by Amicus
P.O. Box 1329, Mankato, MN 56002
www.amicuspublishing.us

Illustrations by Amy Cartwright

Produced for Amicus by The Peterson Publishing Company and Red Line Editorial.

Editor Jenna Gleisner
Designer Craig Hinton
Printed in the United States of America
North Mankato, MN
10 9 8 7 6 5 4 3 2 1

Library of Congress Cataloging-in-Publication Data
Powell, Marie, 1958- author.
   When, Jen? / by Marie Powell ; illustrated by Amy Cartwright.
      pages cm. -- (Word families)
   Summary: "Young readers meet Jen and Ben, who can't seem to gather all of the piglets at the farm, while learning words in the -en word family."
   Audience: K to Grade 3.
   ISBN 978-1-60753-926-1 (hardcover) --
   ISBN 978-1-68151-050-7 (pdf ebook)
   1. English language--Phonetics--Juvenile literature. 2. Vocabulary--Juvenile literature. 3. Reading--Phonetic method. 4. Readers (Primary) I. Cartwright, Amy, illustrator. II. Title.
   PE1135.P69 2015
   428.1--dc23
                                        2015033462

Today Ben visits Jen at the farm.

"When can we see the piglets, Jen?" asks Ben.

"Today, Ben!" says Jen.
Ben and Jen walk down to
the pigpen.

4

"When were they born, Jen?" asks Ben.

"All **ten** were born last week," says Jen.

"But I only see seven,"
says Ben.
"Oh no! I forgot to fasten
the latch," says Jen.

"Listen!" says Ben. "I think I hear them in the garden."

The piglets run from **Jen** and **Ben**. They run right into an **open** pit of mud.

"I caught one!" says Ben.
Just then, the piglet slips
out of his arms.

Jen jumps over the hen.
She gathers all three
piglets in her arms.

"Quick! Open the pen!" says Jen.

"When can we see the baby goats?" asks Ben. "Maybe tomorrow, Ben," says Jen.

Word Family: -en

Word families are groups of words that rhyme and are spelled the same.

Here are the -en words in this book:

Ben	pen
fasten	pigpen
garden	seven
hen	ten
Jen	then
listen	when
open	

Can you spell any other words with -en?